POETS AND PROPHETS

John Milton

MILTON'S POETRY AND

PAMPHLETS

in order of writing and publication

1625
On the death of an infant

1629
Ode on the Morning of Christ's Nativity

1631
L'Allegro *and* Il Penseroso

1632
Sonnet on Shakespeare

1638
Lycidas

1641
Pamphlet Of Reformation

1641-1661
*Many other pamphlets on political and
religious affairs*

1643
Pamphlet Doctrine and Discipline of Divorce

1644
Areopagitica

1645
Poems by Mr John Milton *published
(including most of his sonnets)*

1649
Pamphlet Tenure of Kings and Magistrates

1667
Paradise Lost *published*

1671
Paradise Regained *and* Samson Agonistes *published*

1673
Poems etc. upon Several Occasions by Mr John Milton
published (including some hitherto unpublished)

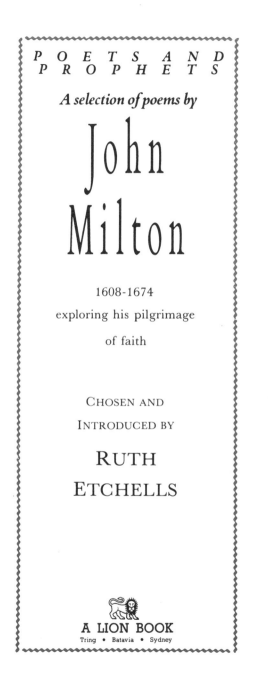

P O E T S A N D
P R O P H E T S

A selection of poems by

John
Milton

1608-1674

exploring his pilgrimage

of faith

CHOSEN AND

INTRODUCED BY

RUTH
ETCHELLS

A LION BOOK

Tring • Batavia • Sydney

Published by
Lion Publishing plc
Icknield Way, Tring, Herts, England
ISBN 0 7459 1388 1
Lion Publishing Corporation
1705 Hubbard Avenue, Batavia, Illinois 60510, USA
ISBN 0 7459 1388 1
Albatross Books Pty Ltd
PO Box 320, Sutherland, NSW 2232, Australia
ISBN 0 86760 927 3

First edition 1988

British Library Cataloguing in Publication Data

Milton, John, *1608-1674*
  Selections from the poetry of John Milton.
  1608-1674.—(Poets and prophets).
  I. Title   II. Etchells, Ruth   III. Series
  821'.4
ISBN 0-7459-1388-1

Library of Congress Cataloging-in-Publication Data

Milton, John, 1608–1674 (Poets and prophets)
  Bibliography: p.
  ISBN 0-7459-1388-1
  1. Christian poetry, English.   I. Etchells, Ruth.   II. Title.
  PR3553.E83   1988
  821'.4—dc19

Printed in Italy

CONTENTS

Introduction   6

O·N·E
Poems of Praise to God   10

Psalm 136   10
Psalm I   13
Ode on the Morning of Christ's Nativity   14
Il Penseroso   17

T·W·O
On Longing to do Great Service for God   18

Sonnet VII   18
Lycidas   19
Sonnet XVI   20

T·H·R·E·E
Faith Amidst the Darkness   21

Sonnet XIX   21
Sonnet XXII   22
Psalm VI   23
Samson Agonistes   24

F·O·U·R
Selections from Paradise Lost   28

The Theme   29
The Enemy   30
The Divine Rescue is Planned   31
On the Edge of Repentance   33
Innocent in Paradise   35
The Change   38
After the Fall   40
The Promise   42
The Beginnings of Reconciliation   44
Into the World   46

Notes   47

INTRODUCTION

$\boxed{\text{B}}$ orn in 1608 in London, into a family of comfortable means—his father was a 'scrivener' (conveyancer)—Milton spent his childhood in Bread Street, Cheapside, the Cheapside of the Mermaid Tavern where Shakespeare was still at that time enjoying good company. The boy was precocious, and his father was ambitious for his learning. He went to St Paul's School, and studied under a headmaster, Alexander Gill, famous as a classical scholar, an authority on the English language, and a theologian. (He was also notable for his brutal discipline.) As a schoolboy at St Paul's, Milton would certainly have attended service in the old St Paul's and sat under the sermons of the great Dean, John Donne.

Milton's passion for classical learning had begun under a tutor even before he attended school, and grew voraciously in his boyhood. He recounts how from the age of twelve he studied almost every night until after midnight: a habit not of weary self-discipline, but of hungry delight which continued in his student days at Cambridge. Together with his facility in classical tongues, it became apparent that he had another, rarer gift: that of poetry.

After a fairly stormy passage at Cambridge during which he was rusticated because of a quarrel with his college tutor, he took his BA degree in March 1629 and his MA in 1632. Between those dates, he had written his first great English poems, 'Ode on the Morning of Christ's Nativity', 'L'Allegro' and 'Il Penseroso'; and his sense that his vocation was to be a great poet was firmly established.

Six years spent at home after his Cambridge days, supported by his father, in private reading (until Spring 1638), years which must have seemed to many, self-indulgent and wasted, since they were leading to no gainful profession, were self-appointed years of 'waiting'. But the waiting was dedicated. Not only was his vision that of writing great poetry; it was of writing great poetry as a *service to God*.

However, the times were requiring of John Milton that he should not merely wait upon his own destiny, but see it in relation to that of his nation. For twenty years he was to put aside the writing of a truly great epic poem in order to publish pamphlets in support of Parliament and the Puritan cause, and to act as Latin Secretary to the Commonwealth Government. He was not to take up again his calling as an epic poet until he was blind, bereaved, and, in the changed political scene which led to the Restoration of the Monarchy, politically disgraced and broken-hearted.

To these difficulties were added those of his marriages. His first marriage, at thirty-three, in 1642, was to a girl of seventeen from a Royalist family. Predictably, yet to his own naïve surprise, it was a disaster: and characteristically his response was to write a series of pamphlets urging the case for the acceptability of divorce. His former Presbyterian associates in the Parliamentary cause were horrified: Milton was seen by many as a 'libertine'.

But Milton was not simply writing out of his own marital need. His views on divorce were not the only matter on which he was to clash with his fellow Puritans. The truth was, his passion for liberty in its profounder sense, was as great, if not greater, than his passion for political and religious reform. Christian 'liberty' was the principle which lay behind his support of Cromwell; Christian liberty was behind his urgings on divorce; and Christian liberty lay behind his increasing attacks on the Presbyterians and the new religious tyranny they were imposing on the nation.

And so John Milton's 'waiting' upon his poetic destiny became one of great personal anguish. His marriage was reconciled in 1645, but his wife died after the birth of their fourth child, in 1652. His infant son, John, died shortly after. And Milton himself became completely blind in that same year. He was forty-three years old: the great poem was still not written, and his sight was gone. He continued up to 1659 as Latin Secretary to the Commonwealth, but dependent on assistance to do the work.

With Cromwell's death in 1658, gathering doubts grew to a head, not simply about the future of the Commonwealth, but about the rights and wrongs of the Revolution which had given it birth. King Charles had been executed on 30 January 1649 in the name of Christian justice. A fortnight later, Milton's first political tract had appeared, written with the aim of reconciling a shaken nation (and world) to that event. All his work for the Puritan Government had had the same purpose. Yet, with the Restoration in 1660 and the desecration of Cromwell's body, John Milton (in hiding from arrest at the time) must have had to face the worst question of all. He had given up the best twenty years of his life to a political ideal now discredited: he had waited fruitlessly through those years for the chance and leisure to write his great projected work. Was all the waiting wasted? Worse: were those who saw King Charles's execution as martyrdom right after all? Had he misunderstood God's will? If not, why had God allowed the disgrace and loss of all he had fought for?

Paradise Lost, which he began to compose in 1657-8 and finished in 1665, is the fruit of his reflection on these anguished questions. His nation's history, and his own, forced him as relentlessly as any circumstances of our own today, to ask how God can be worshipped credibly as both merciful and just. Milton completed in 1658-60 a long Latin treatise, *De Doctrina Christiana*, which expounds his theology systematically. But it is *Paradise Lost*, written out of his own personal grappling with his experience and clothed in the extraordinary richness of his wide reading and daring thinking, which at last emerges as the great poetic epic he had always known as his destiny. It was written with the authority of acute suffering, while yet trusting God: through bereavement (his much-loved second wife, Katherine Woodcock, had died in 1658), through blindness, through public indignity and personal danger.

Yet his closing years (he died in 1674) were happier. He married a third time in 1663: his work was at last widely recognized and his home visited by statesmen and writers of European renown. He suffered acutely from gout, but continued writing up to the end of his life, and survived both the Great Plague of 1665-6 and the Great Fire of London of 1666. Some time before 1671 he composed not only *Paradise Regained* but that greatest of poems of anguished waiting reconciled at last, *Samson Agonistes*. Its closing lines are surely a fitting expression of how Milton came to view a life so full of tragedy and profound disappointment, in which he had nevertheless kept faith with his vision of destiny, his ideal of Christian liberty, his commitment to serve his God and the honour and instruction of his people, and his delight in the good providence of God whose mysterious justice defied understanding and required instead a humble and obedient faith:

> All is best, though we oft doubt,
> What th'unsearchable dispose
> Of Highest Wisdom brings about,
> And ever best found in the close.
> Oft he seems to hide his face,
> But unexpectedly returns
> And to his faithful champion hath in place
> Bore witness gloriously.

POEMS OF PRAISE TO GOD

By the mid-sixteenth century there was already in England a tradition of versifying Psalms, one reason being in order to use them as hymns for singing at worship. Milton's version of Psalm 136 is still in wide use as a hymn today, in different forms. This paraphrase was written when John Milton was fifteen years old, in 1624.

PSALM 136

Let us with a gladsome mind
Praise the Lord, for he is kind;
    For his mercies aye endure,
    Ever faithful, ever sure.

Let us blaze his name abroad,
For of gods he is the God;
    For his, &c.

O let us his praises tell,
Who doth the wrathful tyrants quell;
    For his, &c.

Who with his miracles doth make
Amazed heav'n and earth to shake;
    For his, &c.

Who by his wisdom did create
The painted heav'ns so full of state;
    For his, &c.

Who did the solid earth ordain
To rise above the wat'ry plain;
    For his, &c.

Who by his all-commanding might
Did fill the new-made world with light;
    For his, &c.

And caused the golden-tressèd sun
All the day long his course to run;
   For his, &c.

The hornèd moon to shine by night,
Amongst her spangled sisters bright;
   For his, &c.

He with his thunder-clasping hand
Smote the first-born of Egypt land;
   For his, &c.

And in despite of Pharaoh fell,
He brought from thence his Israel;
   For his, &c.

The ruddy waves he cleft in twain
Of the Erythraean main;
   For his, &c.

The floods stood still like walls of glass,
While the Hebrew bands did pass;
   For his, &c.

But full soon they did devour
The tawny king with all his power;
   For his, &c.

His chosen people he did bless
In the wasteful wilderness;
   For his, &c.

In bloody battle he brought down
Kings of prowess and renown;
   For his, &c.

He foiled bold Seon and his host,
That ruled the Amorrean coast;
   For his, &c.

And large-limbed Og he did subdue,
With all his over-hardy crew;
   For his, &c.

And to his servant Israel
He gave their land therein to dwell;
  For his, &c.

He hath with a piteous eye
Beheld us in our misery;
  For his, &c.

And freed us from the slavery
Of the invading enemy;
  For his, &c.

All living creatures he doth feed,
His mighty majesty and worth;
  For his, &c.

That his mansion hath on high
Above the reach of mortal eye;
  For his mercies aye endure,
  Ever faithful, ever sure.

PSALM I

In 1648, and in 1653, Milton again turned to the versifying of Psalms. An early anonymous biographer said of him that 'David's Psalms were in esteem with him above all poetry'; and it is likely that an exercise which he undertook for the benefit of public worship was, by 1653, also a source of personal comfort to the blind and disappointed poet. By the time he produced the paraphrase of Psalm I (below) he had been blind for at least a year and a half. The tone of faith and praise is the more remarkable.

Blest is the man who hath not walked astray
In counsel of the wicked, and i' th' way
Of sinners hath not stood, and in the seat
Of scorners hath not sat. But in the great
Jehovah's Law is ever his delight,
And in his Law he studies day and night.
He shall be as a tree which planted grows
By wat'ry streams, and in his season knows
To yield his fruit, and his leaf shall not fall,
And what he takes in hand shall prosper all.
Not so the wicked; but as chaff which fanned
The wind drives, so the wicked shall not stand
In judgment, or abide their trial then,
Nor sinners in th' assembly of just men.
For the Lord knows th' upright way of the just,
And the way of bad men to ruin must.

This great poem was written at Christmas, 1629, when Milton was just twenty years old. Its theme is that of praise to God and thankfulness for the Christmas gift of Jesus Christ. It uses some material from the Bible, but expands it with legends and Milton's own fancies. In it Milton ponders on the paradoxical contrast between the helpless Baby and God's divine power. This contrast has meaning for the whole cosmos. In the verses selected below, Nature is waiting for the coming of her Creator, and this is heralded by the music of the angels mingled with the music of the sphere. This reminds Milton of the music of Creation itself; and that takes him forward from the first act of God for his world, creation, to his last act, that of judgement.

Our excerpt from the poem ends here, having ranged from beginning to end of time and space. At the centre of this vast plan is the Incarnation—God become man; his redemption of the world for all eternity. The point of the Christmas story is sharply made: the 'age of gold (Paradise itself) cannot come again simply through the 'holy song' of the angels, it comes through the Babe who 'on the bitter cross must redeem our loss'.

The air such pleasure loth to lose
With thousand echoes still prolongs each heav'nly close.

Nature that heard such sound
Beneath the hollow round
 Of Cynthia's seat, the airy region thrilling,
Now was almost won
To think her part was done,
 And that her reign had here its last fulfilling;
She knew such harmony alone
Could hold all heav'n and earth in happier union.

At last surrounds their sight
A globe of circular light,
　　That with long beams the shamefaced Night arrayed;
The helmèd Cherubim
And sworded Seraphim
　　Are seen in glittering ranks with wings displayed,
Harping in loud and solemn quire
With unexpressive notes to Heaven's new-born heir.

Such music (as 'tis said)
Before was never made,
　　But when of old the sons of morning sung,
While the Creator great
His constellations set,
　　And the well-balanced world on hinges hung,
And cast the dark foundations deep,
And bid the welt'ring waves their oozy channel keep.

Ring out, ye crystal spheres,
Once bless our human ears
　　(If ye have power to touch our senses so),
And let your silver chime
Move in melodious time,
　　And let the bass of heav'n's deep organ blow;
And with your ninefold harmony
Make up full consort to th' angelic symphony.

For if such holy song
Enwrap our fancy long,
　　Time will run back and fetch the age of gold,
And speckled Vanity
Will sicken soon and die,
　　And leprous Sin will melt from earthly mold,
And hell itself will pass away,
And leave her dolorous mansions to the peering day.

Yea, Truth and Justice then
Will down return to men,
   Orbed in a rainbow; and, like glories wearing,
Mercy will sit between,
Throned in celestial sheen,
   With radiant feet the tissued clouds down steering;
And heav'n as at some festival
Will open wide the gates of her high palace hall.

But wisest Fate says no,
This must not yet be so;
   The Babe lies yet in smiling infancy,
That on the bitter cross
Must redeem our loss,
   So both himself and us to glorify;
Yet first, to those ychained in sleep,
The wakeful trump of doom must thunder through the
deep,

With such a horrid clang
As on Mount Sinai rang
   While the red fire and smold'ring clouds outbrake:
The aged Earth, aghast
With terror of that blast,
   Shall from the surface to the centre shake,
When at the world's last session
The dreadful Judge in middle air shall spread his throne.

And then at last our bliss
Full and perfect is,
   But now begins; for from this happy day
Th' old Dragon under ground,
In straiter limits bound,
   Not half so far casts his usurpèd sway,
And wroth to see his kingdom fail,
Swinges the scaly horror of his folded tail.

Milton regularly used images of harmony and discord to picture God's work in a broken and jangling world. His early poem, 'Il Penseroso', contains lines which describe the solace of harmony and its divine power to restore and give new life to his soul.

> To walk the studious cloister's pale,
> And love the high embowèd roof,
> With antique pillars massy proof,
> And storied windows richly dight,
> Casting a dim religious light.
> There let the pealing organ blow
> To the full-voiced quire below,
> In service high and anthems clear,
> As may with sweetness, through mine ear,
> Dissolve me into ecstasies,
> And bring all heav'n before mine eyes.
> And may at last my weary age
> Find out the peaceful hermitage,
> The hairy gown and mossy cell,
> Where I may sit and rightly spell
> Of every star that heav'n doth shew,
> And every herb that sips the dew,
> Till old experience do attain
> To something like prophetic strain.

ON LONGING TO DO GREAT SERVICE FOR GOD

O n his twenty-fourth birthday (9 December 1632), Milton was studying at home, his Cambridge career behind him. The sonnet below describes his fellow students forging ahead in careers of active service, while his own vocation remains unfulfilled and obscure. Nevertheless, through these years of preparation, he remains committed to his sense of high calling, and re-dedicates himself to whatever great service God has for him.

SONNET VII

How soon hath Time, the subtle thief of youth,
   Stol'n on his wing my three and twentieth year!
   My hasting days fly on with full career,
   But my late spring no bud or blossom shew'th.
Perhaps my semblance might deceive the truth,
   That I to manhood am arrived so near,
And inward ripeness doth much less appear,
That some more timely-happy spirits endu'th.
Yet be it less or more, or soon or slow,
   It shall be still in strictest measure ev'n
   To that same lot, however mean or high,
Toward which Time leads me, and the will of Heav'n;
   All is, if I have grace to use it so,
As ever in my great Task-Master's eye.

Some of Milton's most moving lines about his own sense of destiny and his dreams of 'immortal fame', can be found in his poem 'Lycidas', written a month before his twenty-ninth birthday in 1637. This poem was written for a volume of elegies in honour of Edward King, a graduate of Milton's own Cambridge college, Christ's. Edward King had been drowned in a shipwreck in the Irish Sea, and his sudden death causes Milton to reflect on how vulnerable to disaster human life is. Yet fame is not so easily destroyed—particularly if it is the honour given by God Himself to a life of obedience which is glorious in its humbleness.

Fame is the spur that the clear spirit doth raise
(That last infirmity of noble mind)
To scorn delights, and live laborious days;
But the fair guerdon when we hope to find,
And think to burst out into sudden blaze,
Comes the blind Fury with th' abhorrèd shears,
And slits the thin-spun life. 'But not the praise,'
Phoebus replied, and touched my trembling ears:
'Fame is no plant that grows on mortal soil,
Nor in the glistering foil
Set off to th' world, nor in broad rumor lies,
But lives and spreads aloft by those pure eyes
And perfect witness of all-judging Jove;
As he pronounces lastly on each deed,
Of so much fame in heav'n expect thy meed.'

S ome of Milton's sharpest lines in 'Lycidas' refer to the corruption and incompetence of the clergy, those 'blind mouths' whom Milton saw as false herdsmen, like the 'hireling shepherds' of the Bible, to whom the hungry sheep look, yet are not fed!

Nearly fifteen years later, Milton is still fighting the cause of integrity among religious leaders. In Sonnet XVI, written in 1652, he appeals to the Lord General Cromwell to defend religious liberty, not this time from the 'wolves' of the Roman Catholic Church (as in 'Lycidas') but from the powerful Independent sect which was proposing to create a new state Church on the Congregational model. For Milton this is another example of corrupt Christian leaders failing in their responsibility to those they should be serving, and in the process destroying Christian freedom.

Cromwell, our chief of men, who through a cloud
   Not of war only, but detractions rude,
   Guided by faith and matchless fortitude
To peace and truth thy glorious way hast ploughed,
And on the neck of crownèd Fortune proud
   Hast reared God's trophies and his work pursued,
   While Darwen stream, with blood of Scots imbrued,

And Dunbar field resounds thy praises loud,
And Worcester's laureate wreath; yet much remains
   To conquer still: peace hath her victories
   No less renowned than war; new foes arise
Threat'ning to bind our souls with secular chains.
   Help us to save free conscience from the paw
   Of hireling wolves whose gospel is their maw.

FAITH AMIDST THE DARKNESS

In the winter of 1651-52, approaching his forty-third birthday, Milton became completely blind. His sight had been failing for some time, and by early 1650 he had already almost totally lost the sight of one eye. Though warned about the effect of continued over-exertion, he persevered in his arduous task of writing in defence of the execution of Charles I and of Cromwell's Commonwealth. The two sonnets below were written out of the crisis of faith he had to face. He was blind, and he had not yet written the great epic poem he was sure was his calling. What comfort could he find? In Sonnet XIX (as in Sonnet VII above) the parable of the talents recorded in the New Testament is running through his mind: now it seems to confront him with a task not done. Yet he remains steadfast in his conviction that his life and work are in God's hand.

SONNET XIX

When I consider how my light is spent,
   Ere half my days, in this dark world and wide,
   And that one talent which is death to hide
   Lodged with me useless, though my soul more bent
To serve therewith my Maker, and present
   My true account, lest he returning chide,
   'Doth God exact day-labor, light denied?'
   I fondly ask. But Patience, to prevent
That murmur, soon replies: 'God doth not need
   Either man's work or his own gifts; who best
   Bear his mild yoke, they serve him best. His state
Is kingly: thousands at his bidding speed,
   And post o'er land and ocean without rest;
   They also serve who only stand and wait.

Three years later, Milton is still struggling with the same questions; but by now he can point to certain achievements in his long service to the Commonwealth. He has published his first and second *Defence of the English People* (1651, 1654). And it comforts him to know that his sight has been lost 'in liberty's defense': it has been a 'noble task of which all Europe talks from side to side'. So he will not lose heart or hope, or 'argue against Heaven's hand'. He is 'content, though blind'.

Cyriack, this three years' day these eyes, though clear
    To outward view of blemish or of spot,
    Bereft of light their seeing have forgot;
Nor to their idle orbs doth sight appear
Of sun or moon or star throughout the year,
    Or man or woman. Yet I argue not
    Against Heav'n's hand or will, nor bate a jot
Of heart or hope, but still bear up and steer
Right onward. What supports me, dost thou ask?
    The conscience, friend, to have lost them overplied
    In liberty's defense, my noble task,
Of which all Europe talks from side to side.
    This thought might lead me through the world's vain
      masque,
    Content though blind, had I no better guide.

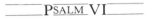

[A] nother psalm versified in this period indicates the suffering out of which Milton is making his great affirmations of faith. In 1653 he wrote fresh rhyming versions, much more experimental in metre than previously, of Psalms 1 to 8. The images he develops in these relate powerfully to his personal circumstances: nowhere is this more marked than in Psalm VI below, particularly lines 13, 14 and 15.

Lord, in thine anger do not reprehend me,
    Nor in thy hot displeasure me correct;
Pity me, Lord, for I am much deject,
    Am very weak and faint; heal and amend me,
For all my bones, that even with anguish ache,
    Are troubled, yea, my soul is troubled sore.
And thou, O Lord, how long? turn, Lord, restore
    My soul, O save me for thy goodness sake,
For in death no remembrance is of thee;
    Who in the grave can celebrate thy praise?
Wearied I am with sighing out my days,
    Nightly my couch I make a kind of sea;
My bed I water with my tears; mine eye
    Through grief consumes, is waxen old and dark
I' th' midst of all mine enemies that mark.
    Depart, all ye that work iniquity.
Depart from me, for the voice of my weeping
    The Lord hath heard; the Lord hath heard my prayer;
My supplication with acceptance fair
    The Lord will own, and have me in his keeping.
Mine enemies shall all be blank and dashed
    With much confusion; then grow red with shame;
They shall return in haste the way they came
    And in a moment shall be quite abashed.

SAMSON AGONISTES

$\boxed{T}$ he traditional view of the order in which Milton produced his work suggests that his last poem was *Samson Agonistes*. It was written almost certainly between 1660 and 1670 (published with *Paradise Regained* in 1671). It reveals an attitude of steady composure and certain conviction about the goodness and final authority of God's wisdom in ordering the world—the very core of Milton's hardwon faith achieved in the face of the dissolution of all his hopes with the Restoration of Monarchy.

In his poem *Samson Agonistes*, Milton uses the biblical story of Samson to explore the theme of God's justice. He structures the poem as a Greek tragedy, though not for the stage. And in it he subjects Samson, the hero— now a blind and disgraced slave to the Philistines whom God had called him to defeat—to various temptations. But though Samson, like Adam, at the end of *Paradise Lost* is fallen, yet we see his recovery and his victory in the name of his God, not just over his enemies, but over himself. Hence the calm certainty of the poem's closing lines.

In our first selection of lines from *Samson Agonistes*, the chorus is reflecting on the theme of the justice of God's ways, even though it is often hard for us to recognize them as just.

> *Chor.* Just are the ways of God
> And justifiable to men;
> Unless there be who think not God at all:
> If any be, they walk obscure;
> For of such doctrine never was there school,
> But the heart of the fool,
> And no man therein doctor but himself.
> Yet more there be who doubt his ways not just,
> As to his own edicts, found contradicting,
> Then give the reins to wand'ring thought,
> Regardless of his glory's diminution;
> Till by their own perplexities involved
> They ravel more, still less resolved,
> But never find self-satisfying solution
> As if they would confine th'Interminable,
> And tie him to his own prescript,
> Who made our laws to bind us, not himself,
> And hath full right to exempt
> Whomso it pleases him by choice
> From national obstruction, without taint
> Of sin, or legal debt;
> For with his own laws he can best dispense...

Lines 293-314

To his affirmation of God's justice Milton adds, in the statements of Samson, an acknowledgement of human sinfulness and the punishment it justly deserves. Nevertheless, Samson believes in God's final gracious pardoning.

Sam. All these indignities, for such they are
From thine, these evils I deserve and more,
Acknowledge them from God inflicted on me
Justly, yet despair not of his final pardon
Whose ear is ever open, and his eye
Gracious to readmit the suppliant...

Lines 1168-1173

$\boxed{A}$ t the end of the poem the Messenger brings Samson's father and friends the news that Samson has pulled down the pillars of the Philistine temple and killed both the Philistines and himself. Their response is profound thankfulness that Samson has recovered not only his bodily strength but that moral fervour which made him so powerful in the battles against God's enemies. In this presentation of the story, Samson—blind and disgraced as Milton himself had been—is permitted one last great deed for God, which vindicates God's honour and restores his own sense of value in God's service. Samson's father speaks of Samson's last great act and how it may be interpreted with the eye of faith.

And which is best and happiest yet, all this
With God not parted from him, as was feared,
But favoring and assisting to the end.
Nothing is here for tears, nothing to wail
Or knock the breast, no weakness, no contempt,
Dispraise, or blame; nothing but well and fair,
And what may quiet us in a death so noble.

Chor. All is best, though we oft doubt,
What th' unsearchable dispose
Of highest wisdom brings about,
And ever best found in the close.
Oft he seems to hide his face,
But unexpectedly returns
And to his faithful Champion hath in place
Bore witness gloriously; whence Gaza mourns
And all that band them to resist
His uncontroulable intent
His servants he with new acquist
Of true experience from this great event
With peace and consolation hath dismist,
And calm of mind all passion spent.

Lines 1718-1724 and 1745 to the end

SELECTIONS FROM
PARADISE LOST

Messiah crowned, God's reconciled decree,
Rebelling angels, the forbidden tree,
Heaven, hell, earth, chaos, all...

The majesty which through thy work doth reign
Draws the devout, deterring the profane.

Andrew Marvell, Preface to
Paradise Lost, 2nd edition, 1674

$\boxed{\text{S}}$ oon after Milton's return from Italy in 1639, when he was thirty-one years old, he listed nearly a hundred possible subjects for a drama, probably epic in style, some biblical, some legendary, some historical. Four outlines followed, each of them amplifying a possible epic treatment of the story of Adam and Eve. The world's history, to which this story is central, is presented wholly in terms of God's relationship with the world, through the context of certain key acts: God's creation of the world, its creatures and humankind; Mankind's fall and its consequences; the divine rescue of the world through the life, death and resurrection of Christ; and the anticipated end of the world and its judgement on the Last Day.

Through this study of the history of the world in relationship to God, Milton is facing the hard questions he had confronted in his own life, and which grip our own generation no less painfully. How is it possible to talk credibly of a God who is both loving and just? Why must humanity suffer so? What is the cause of evil? Why do things, even well-intentioned, go wrong? Is God in charge? Why must we wait so long for a sign?

Milton sets God's acts in relation to the world in the

vaster context of his absolute rule over all that is, so the story of Adam and Eve becomes the focus for the drama of the war between God and the forces which oppose him, led by the fallen Archangel, Satan. We are taken back to Satan's first disobedience and its consequences. Humankind's present sorry state is seen as the local reflection and outcome of this.

Yet there is comfort. For, even though the story is of the loss of Paradise, it is also the story of God's willingness to pay whatever it may cost in order to secure the ultimate good of humankind.

THE THEME
Book I, lines 1-10, 22-26

Milton sets out briefly the story he is to tell, and prays for inspiration in his task, that he may affirm the justice and goodness of God.

> Of Man's first disobedience, and the fruit
> Of that forbidden tree, whose mortal taste
> Brought death into the world, and all our woe,
> With loss of Eden, till one greater Man
> Restore us, and regain the blissful seat,
> Sing, Heav'nly Muse, that on the secret top
> Of Oreb, or of Sinai, didst inspire
> That shepherd who first taught the chosen seed
> In the beginning how the heav'ns and earth
> Rose out of Chaos;...
>   what in me is dark
> Illumines what is low raise and support;
> That to the highth of this great argument
> I may assert Eternal Providence,
> And justify the ways of God to men.

⬚S⬚ atan and the rebel angels, defeated in their attempt to take heaven by force, have been flung out of heaven and find themselves in the fiery lake of hell. Unrepentant, though appalled, Satan, the 'lost Archangel' declares his defiance, and his total refusal to accept the authority of God. Instead, he will make his own kingdom here, since 'fardest from him is best'. In desiring to be as far away from God as possible, Satan reaches the opposite conclusion about the true and best source of comfort from the conclusion Adam will reach when he too has to face the consequences of disobeying God. Satan boasts of 'a mind not to be changed': Adam, by contrast, is deeply penitent.

> 'Is this the region, this the soil, the clime,'
> Said then the lost Archangel, 'this the seat
> That we must change for heav'n, this mournful gloom
> For that celestial light? Be it so, since he
> Who now is sovran can dispose and bid
> What shall be right: fardest from him is best,
> Whom reason hath equaled, force hath made supreme
> Above his equals. Farewell, happy fields,
> Where joy for ever dwells! Hail, horrors, hail,
> Infernal world, and thou, profoundest hell,
> Receive thy new possessor: one who brings
> A mind not to be changed by place or time.
> The mind is its own place, and in itself
> Can make a heav'n of hell, a hell of heav'n...'

Book III, lines 203-216, 232-252

I n heaven Satan's journey to earth is known, his purpose understood, and its success sadly recognized. God
pronounces the terrible truth of absolute justice: if
mankind is not required to face the consequences of
disobedience and disloyalty, then the fabric of order, law
and justice is destroyed: 'Die he or justice must.' Yet this
terrible sanction may be overcome if there is one willing
to pay the price of justice by taking upon himself the
inevitable consequences of wrongdoing. God asks if any
will undertake a task of such love and sacrifice. And
Milton proposes a volunteer. God's only Son, in offering to step in between justice and wrong, foretells that
by so doing he will break for ever the chain of consequence
resulting from sin. Thus he will destroy the power of
Satan's most powerful tool, Death.

Man disobeying,
Disloyal breaks his fealty, and sins
Against the high supremacy of Heav'n,
Affecting Godhead, and so losing all,
To expiate his treason hath naught left,
But to destruction sacred and devote,
He with his whole posterity must die;
Die he or justice must; unless for him
Some other able, and as willing, pay
The rigid satisfaction, death for death.
Say, heav'nly Powers, where shall we find such love?
Which of ye will be mortal to redeem
Man's mortal crime, and just th' unjust to save?
Dwells in all heaven charity so dear?...

Father, thy word is passed, man shall find grace;
And shall grace not find means, that finds her way,
The speediest of thy wingèd messengers,
To visit all thy creatures, and to all
Comes unprevented, unimplored, unsought?

Happy for man, so coming; he her aid
Can never seek, once dead in sins and lost;
Atonement for himself or offering meet,
Indebted and undone, hath none to bring.
Behold me then, me for him, life for life
I offer; on me let thine anger fall;
Account me man; I for his sake will leave
Thy bosom, and this glory next to thee
Freely put off, and for him lastly die
Well pleased; on me let Death wreck all his rage;
Under his gloomy power I shall not long
Lie vanquished; thou hast giv'n me to possess
Life in myself for ever; by thee I live;
Though now to Death I yield, and am his due,
All that of me can die, yet that debt paid,
Thou wilt not leave me in the loathsome grave
His prey, nor suffer my unspotted soul
For ever with corruption there to dwell;
But I shall rise victorious, and subdue
My vanquisher, spoiled of his vaunted spoil;
Death his death's wound shall then receive, and stoop
Inglorious, of his mortal sting disarmed.

T̲he consequence of Satan's determination never to admit himself in the wrong is that he plots revenge by attacking God's latest and best-loved creation, the Earth, and especially those two creatures most precious to God, man and woman, Adam and Eve. Satan therefore makes the perilous journey from hell to earth. But when he arrives there the world's beauty is so great that, looking at it, for a moment he glimpses what he once was—and half begins to repent:

>   horror and doubt distract
> His troubled thoughts, and from the bottom stir
> The hell within him, for within him hell
> He brings, and round about him, nor from hell
> One step no more than from himself can fly
> By change of place. Now conscience wakes despair
> That slumbered, wakes the bitter memory
> Of what he was, what is, and what must be
> Worse; of worse deeds worse sufferings must ensue.

Briefly he confronts the truth. His present awful condition is a matter wholly of his own choice, and it seems he cannot escape it, for hell is his very self and he carries it with him wherever he goes. Is there no relenting, no pardon? There *is* a way: but it would require his submission to God as Lord; and that he will not bring himself to consider, for it would mean humbling himself. Therefore he will reject remorse, and for ever make evil his good:

>   Whom hast thou then or what to accuse,
> But Heav'n's free love dealt equally to all?
> Be then his love accurst, since love or hate,
> To me alike, it deals eternal woe.
> Nay cursed be thou, since against his thy will
> Chose freely what it now so justly rues.

Me miserable! which way shall I fly
Infinite wrath, and infinite despair?
Which way I fly is hell; myself am hell;
And in the lowest deep a lower deep
Still threat'ning to devour me opens wide,
To which the hell I suffer seems a heav'n.
O then at last relent: is there no place
Left for repentance, none for pardon left?
None left but by submission; and that word
Disdain forbids me, and my dread of shame
Among the Spirits beneath...
So farewell hope, and with hope farewell fear,
Farewell remorse! All good to me is lost;
Evil, be thou my good; by thee at least
Divided empire with heav'n's King I hold
By thee, and more than half perhaps will reign;
As man ere long, and this new world shall know.

Book IV, lines 288-311, 321-324, 340-365, 724-735

M ilton does not dodge the nearly-impossible task of por-
traying innocence and perfection in humanity's golden
age by suggesting it simply through Satan's envy. Instead
he presents a delightful picture not only of Adam and Eve
themselves, but of their paradisal world. In it there are
gentle flashes of humour in the glimpses of the animals.
Again, however, we catch sight of Satan in agony, as he
sees 'undelighted, all delight', attracted to it by all those
instincts which once were noble, yet hating it because it
is beautiful and he, by his own choice, no longer is so.

    Two of far nobler shape erect and tall,
God-like erect, with native honor clad
In naked majesty seemed lords of all,
And worthy seemed, for in their looks divine
The image of their glorious Maker shone,
Truth, wisdom, sanctitude severe and pure,
Severe but in true filial freedom placed;
Whence true authority in men; though both
Not equal, as their sex not equal seemed;
For contemplation he and valor formed,
For softness she and sweet attractive grace;
He for God only, she for God in him.
His fair large front and eye sublime declared
Absolute rule; and hyacinthine locks
Round from his parted forelock manly hung
Clust'ring, but not beneath his shoulders broad:
She as a veil down to the slender waist
Her unadornèd golden tresses wore
Disheveled, but in wanton ringlets waved
As the vine curls her tendrils, which implied
Subjection, but required with gentle sway,
And by her yielded, by him best received,
Yielded with coy submission, modest pride,
And sweet reluctant amorous delay...
So hand in hand they passed, the loveliest pair

That ever since in love's embraces met,
Adam the goodliest man of men since born
His sons, the fairest of her daughters Eve...
    About them frisking played
All beasts of th' earth, since wild, and of all chase
In wood or wilderness, forest or den;
Sporting the lion ramped, and in his paw
Dandled the kid; bears, tigers, ounces, pards,
Gamboled before them; th' unwieldy elephant
To make them mirth used all his might, and wreathed
His lithe proboscis; close the serpent sly
Insinuating, wove with Gordian twine
His braided train, and of his fatal guile
Gave proof unheeded; others on the grass
Couched, and now filled with pasture gazing sat,
Or bedward ruminating; for the sun
Declined was hasting now with prone career
To th' ocean isles, and in th' ascending scale
Of heav'n the stars that usher evening rose:
When Satan still in gaze, as first he stood,
Scarce thus at length failed speech recovered sad:
    'Oh hell! what do mine eyes with grief behold!
Into our room of bliss thus high advanced
Creatures of other mold, earth-born perhaps,
Not Spirits, yet to heav'nly Spirits bright
Little inferior; whom my thoughts pursue
With wonder, and could love, so lively shines
In them divine resemblance, and such grace
The hand that formed them on their shape hath
poured...'

This glimpse of creation before the fall is given a focus in the spontaneous worship of Adam and Eve of their Father Creator, in their evening hymn, as the evening described in the lines above turns into night:

> 'Thou also mad'st the night,
> Maker Omnipotent, and thou the day,
> Which we in our appointed work employed
> Have finished happy in our mutual help
> And mutual love, the crown of all our bliss
> Ordained by thee, and this delicious place
> For us too large, where thy abundance wants
> Partakers, and uncropped falls to the ground.
> But thou hast promised from us two a race
> To fill the earth, who shall with us extol
> Thy goodness infinite, both when we wake,
> And when we seek, as now, thy gift of sleep.'

The dreadful change in humanity's history begins in the epic in Book IX, and Milton focuses it, as always, most crucially in what is to happen in the relationship between mankind and God. The lovely trust and serenity celebrated, for instance, in the lines of the Evening Hymn above, must be replaced by 'foul distrust' and 'revolt and disobedience' on mankind's part, and 'anger and just rebuke' on the part of heaven: alienation and 'distance' are to be the keynote of what follows:

No more of talk where God or angel guest
With man, as with his friend, familiar used
To sit indulgent, and with him partake
Rural repast, permitting him the while
Venial discourse unblamed. I now must change
Those notes to tragic; foul distrust, and breach
Disloyal on the part of man, revolt,
And disobedience; on the part of Heav'n
Now alienated, distance and distaste,
Anger and just rebuke, and judgment giv'n,
That brought into this world a world of woe,
Sin and her shadow Death, and misery,
Death's harbinger. Sad task, yet argument
Not less but more heroic.

Book X, lines 710-725, 754-759, 766-770,
817-818, 822-828

|O| ne of the most powerful expressions of humanity's act
of disengagement from God is its effect on Paradise. But
even deeper are its consequences for Adam, who in agony
of mind speaks from a 'troubled sea of passion' the
thoughts that pain him most. Why should God make such
a fuss over such a small action? Yet honesty compels
Adam to admit that he had never questioned the conditions God placed on his happiness; so to challenge the
terms of the contract after breaking it can carry little
weight in justice. Moreover, God had the right to do what
he chose with what he had made: Adam was simply his
creature.

Beast now with beast gan war, and fowl with fowl,
And fish with fish; to graze the herb all leaving,
Devour'd each other; nor stood much in awe
Of man, but fled him, or with count'nance grim
Glared on him passing. These were from without
The growing miseries, which Adam saw
Already in part, though hid in gloomiest shade,
To sorrow abandoned, but worse felt within,
And in a troubled sea of passion tossed,
Thus to disburden sought with sad complaint:
　'O miserable of happy! Is this the end
Of this new glorious world, and me so late
The glory of that glory, who now, become
Accurst of blessèd, hide me from the face
Of God, whom to behold was then my highth
Of happiness?...

　　　　　　　　　　　　　　Inexplicable
Why justice seems; yet to say truth, too late
I thus contest; then should have been refused
Those terms whatever, when they were proposed.
Thou didst accept them; wilt thou enjoy the good,
Then cavil the conditions?...

God made thee of choice his own, and of his own
To serve him; thy reward was of his grace;
Thy punishment then justly is at his will.
Be it so, for I submit, his doom is fair,
That dust I am, and shall to dust return...'

THE PROMISE

Book XI, lines 315-323, 327-333, 340-342, 349-354
Book XII, lines 469-478, 561-563, 575-587

Adam and Eve are not left alone to face unaided the consequences of their fractured relationship with God. The Archangel Michael is sent to show them all that is to happen, up to the victorious moment of Christ's crucifixion and the freeing of humankind from the endless chain of sin's consequence. To begin with, Adam's response to the decree of banishment from Paradise is one of great distress. But Michael reassures him. God will be present wherever they go 'still compassing thee round with goodness and paternal love':

'This most afflicts me, that departing hence,
As from his face I shall be hid, deprived
His blessed count'nance; here I could frequent,
With worship, place by place where he vouchsafed
Presence Divine, and to my sons relate:
"On this mount he appeared, under this tree
Stood visible, among these pines his voice
I heard, here with him at this fountain talked."...
In yonder nether world where shall I seek
His bright appearances, or footstep trace?
For though I fled him angry, yet recalled
To life prolonged and promised race, I now
Gladly behold though but his utmost skirts
Of glory, and far off his steps adore.'
                              '...Surmise not then
His presence to these narrow bounds confined
Of Paradise or Eden:...
Yet doubt not but in valley and in plain
God is as here, and will be found alike
Present, and of his presence many a sign
Still following thee, still compassing thee round
With goodness and paternal love, his face
Express, and of his steps the track divine...'

Perhaps the most poignant misery Adam feels is that he has called down this pain not only on himself but on all the generations to come:

Nor I on my part single; in me all
Posterity stands cursed.
                     Ah, why should all mankind
For one man's fault thus guiltless be condemned,
If guiltless? But from me what can proceed
But all corrupt, both mind and will depraved,
Not to do only, but to will the same
With me? How can they then acquitted stand
In sight of God?

THE BEGINNINGS OF RECONCILIATION:
ADAM WITH EVE
Book X, lines 958-965

A t the centre of this great misery is the rupture between Adam and Eve. Adam has turned away from her in complete alienation. She pleads with him to accept her penitence, longing to take the full consequences to herself. What follows is written from Milton's own marital reconciliation. For, touched to the heart by her real grief, Adam then draws her to him, in reconciliation and forgiveness:

> But rise, let us no more contend, nor blame
> Each other, blamed enough elsewhere, but strive
> In offices of love, how we may light'n
> Each other's burden in our share of woe;
> Since this day's death denounced, if aught I see,
> Will prove no sudden, but a slow-paced evil,
> A long day's dying to augment our pain,
> And to our seed (O hapless seed!) derived.

Adam's own comfort is secured by the promise that God will save Adam's descendants from the full consequence of Adam's act. He then bursts out in wonder and relief and deep thankfulness:

> O goodness infinite, goodness immense!
> That all this good of evil shall produce,
> And evil turn to good; more wonderful
> Than that which by creation first brought forth
> Light out of darkness! Full of doubt I stand,
> Whether I should repent me now of sin
> By me done and occasioned, or rejoice
> Much more, that much more good thereof shall spring,
> To God more glory, more good will to men
> From God, and over wrath grace shall abound...
> Henceforth I learn that to obey is best,
> And love with fear the only God, to walk
> As in his presence, ever to observe

His providence, and on him sole depend,
Merciful over all his works, with good
Still overcoming evil, and by small
Accomplishing great things, by things deemed weak
Subverting worldly strong, and worldly wise
By simply meek; that suffering for truth's sake
Is fortitude to highest victory,
And to the faithful death the gate of life;
Taught this by his example whom I now
Acknowledge my Redeemer ever blest.

The Archangel declares that Adam has at last understood the nature of real wisdom and made it his own. And just as Satan carried with him the hell that was his own state, so Adam and Eve would for ever possess within themselves a paradise fairer even than the one they must leave:

This having learnt, thou hast attained the sum
Of wisdom; hope no higher, though all the stars
Thou knew'st by name, and all th' ethereal powers,
All secrets of the deep, all Nature's works,
Or works of God in heav'n, air, earth, or sea,
And all the riches of this world enjoy'dst,
And all the rule, one empire; only add
Deeds to thy knowledge answerable, add faith,
Add virtue, patience, temperance, add love,
By name to come called charity, the soul
Of all the rest: then wilt thou not be loth
To leave this Paradise, but shalt possess
A paradise within thee, happier far.

Into the World
Book XII, lines 641-649

But now the reality of their eviction from Paradise must be faced, and Milton must bring his Adam and Eve to join his readers in their present unparadised state of waiting: waiting, thankfully, for the mercy of Christ's loving act in securing their ultimate safety, but weary with longing for the fulfilment of that release from the bondage of a suffering earth. With that ahead, Milton sounds a note of loss, but of faith: the characteristic note which had sounded through his own long pilgrimage:

They, looking back, all th' eastern side beheld
Of Paradise, so late their happy seat,
Waved over by that flaming brand, the gate
With dreadful faces thronged and fiery arms.
Some natural tears they dropped, but wiped them soon;
The world was all before them, where to choose
Their place of rest, and Providence their guide:
They hand in hand, with wand'ring steps and slow,
Through Eden took their solitary way.

NOTES

Page 10
Psalm 136, paraphrase
Milton's father was himself an amateur composer, and had contributed some tunes in the *Whole Book of Psalms* published by Thomas Ravenscroft in 1621. This was the background to John Milton's early attempts, in 1624 when he was fifteen years old, to paraphrase Psalms. (Another example is his version of Psalm 114.)

Page 13
Psalm 1
It is worth noticing that Milton has used a much more experimental metre and rhyme scheme here than in his youthful versions. He had produced nine versified psalms five years earlier, in 1648, and this psalm is one of a group—Psalms 1-8—'done into verse' at one of the darkest periods of his life. (See Introduction.)

Page 14
'Ode on the Morning of Christ's Nativity'
Milton's first great English poem: the stanza form is almost certainly Milton's own invention. In his *Poems* of 1645, Milton placed this poem first.

Page 17
'Il Penseroso'
This poem was probably written when Milton was 22, in his last long Cambridge vacation. It is linked by parallels and contrasts to 'L'Allegro'. Both poems owe much to a formal literary convention.

Page 18
Sonnet VII, 'How soon with Time...'
In a letter to a friend, almost certainly his old tutor, Thomas Young, Milton responds to the challenge that his life of study is self-indulgent. He still feels he should be prepared to make his life-offering late, 'so it gave advantage to be more fit', but acknowledges the anxieties he feels from time to time about his own delays in producing great work: and quotes this sonnet as proof of the way he has faced these anxieties.

Page 19
'Lycidas'
This poem was included in a volume in honour of Edward King, a former student of Christ's College. Its main argument is that such accidental death cannot be outside the will of God: and therefore the question of why the innocent and good should suffer becomes a movement towards affirmation of faith. The poem moves through the various forms of suffering, from the violence of nature to human hypocrisy, but emerges in one of Milton's great serene endings.

Page 20
Sonnet XVI
The full manuscript title is 'To the Lord General Cromwell, May, 1652, on the proposals of certain ministers at the Committee for Propagation of the Gospel'.

Page 21
Sonnet XIX
There is much argument about the dating of this sonnet (the only text of it is in that of the *Poems* of 1673). The inner evidence suggests it records Milton's first anguished reaction to becoming totally blind, which occurred in the winter of 1651-52.

Page 22

Sonnet XXII

By contrast with Sonnet XIX above, this sonnet dates itself in its first line as 1654-55.

Page 23

Psalm VI

Another versification from his blindness.

Page 24

Samson Agonistes

'Agonistes' has the Greek meaning of 'contestant' and 'actor' and a further suggestion of 'God's champion'. Milton introduces the poem with a brief note on 'that sort of dramatic poem which is called trajedy'. In it he quotes Aristotle on the moral power of trajedy:

'Trajedy, as it was anciently composed, hath been ever held the gravest, moralest, and most profitable of all other poems: therefore said by Aristotle to be of power, by raising pity and fear, or terror, to purge the mind of those and suchlike passions, that is, to temper and reduce them to just measure with a kind of delight, stirred up by reading or seeing those passions well imitated. Heretofore men in highest dignity have labored not a little to be thought able to compose a trajedy.'

Page 28

Paradise Lost

Probably begun during 1657-58, this great poem was complete by summer 1665, and published in 1667 as a poem in ten books, on sale *in toto* for three shillings. In the second edition of 1674 (the year he died) Milton divided each of the original Books 7 and 10 into two, making 12 books in all. His method was to compose at night, so that in the morning his amanuensis (a reluctant daughter) might 'milk' him (his own phrase). We may picture him in his favourite posture for composition, one leg thrown over the arm of his chair, his blind eyes (which showed no sign of blindness to the observer) gazing into the middle distance. The feat of memory alone involved in achieving this epic poem while never seeing a single line of it, is remarkable. His primary sense of it would be that of *hearing*, and this helps to explain the marvellous music of its lines.